WOOD-ENGRAVING AND WOODCUTS

"HOW TO DO IT" SERIES

WOOD-ENGRAVING AND WOODCUTS

By Clare Leighton

"HOW TO DO IT"

SERIES NO. 2

THE STUDIO PUBLICATIONS
LONDON AND NEW YORK

First Published 1932
Reprinted 1932
New Edition 1944
Reprinted 1948

ACKNOWLEDGMENTS

The thanks of the author and publishers are due to all the artists who kindly gave permission to reproduce their prints; also to Mr. Douglas Cleverdon for the use of *Self-Portrait* by Eric Gill. The photographs showing the method of wood-engraving were made by Mr. Cyril Jenkins. Special acknowledgment is also given to the Baltimore Museum of Art for loaning many of their prints for reproduction.

Printed in Great Britain by William Clowes & Sons, Ltd., London and Beccles; and published in London by The Studio Ltd., 66 Chandos Place, W.C.2, and in New York by The Studio Publications Inc., 381 Fourth Avenue.

CONTENTS

ILLUSTRATIONS OF METHOD

EXAMPLES OF WOOD-ENGRAVING & WOODCUTS

INTRODUCTION

Of all media, wood-engraving is the one in which there is the least to be taught and the most to be learnt. The principle of the modern woodcut is that of a white chalk drawing on a blackboard, while the principle of etching is that of a black line drawing on white paper. Every cut made on a wood block prints white, so that the artist is always working up from the black towards the light. If the new, unengraved block were printed, it would be but a rectangle of black ink.

The technique of the wood block has changed radically since the days of the pioneers. The early prints, which should be called woodcuts rather than wood-engravings, nearly always gave the effect of black lines on white, but the white line on a black background is the natural and more direct method. All black line work requires the less spontaneous, more laboured process of cutting away the surface of the wood on both sides of the line to be left black. Occasionally a block is printed intaglio as a curiosity—that is, the ink is pressed *into* the lines cut, and wiped—but the accepted process is a matter of surface printing, such as is used for type.

Materials. The materials needed are simple and fairly inexpensive. I will describe them under separate headings.

Blocks. For wood-engraving these are preferably of boxwood, though apple or pear are possible materials. The section of the wood is used and is cut into thicknesses of about one inch—that is, " type high "—so that it may be used in conjunction with type for books. This top grain gives the engraver complete freedom from splitting or roughness of any sort, enabling him to draw the finest and most diversified lines. For woodcuts, the wood used is softer and along the grain, and any smooth-grained wood will do, such as lime, cherry, American whitewood or maple. For lino-cuts, which are really the same thing in method as woodcuts, ordinary smooth household linoleum is used.

Tools.   Although time can be saved by having a greater variety with many graded sizes, yet only three tools are necessary—the scorper, the graver, and the spitzsticker.   The following are their uses, adding a few extra tools that are undoubtedly good to have :

Scorper.   For cutting out large surfaces or making thick cuts of any sort.

Graver.   For any fine straight line or specks.

Spitzsticker.   For any curved lines.

Square scorper.   For corners ; useful in lettering, also for thick white lines.

Flat chisel tool.   For shaving off any upstanding points of wood from a large cut away surface.

Tint tool.   For finest white lines.

Multiple tool.   A very dangerous tool, apt to make the work look cleverer than it is and mechanical.   Useful for even greys.

For woodcuts on soft wood or linoleum, an ordinary knife can be used, but as this requires that two cuts should be made—each downwards and slanted towards each other—in order to get a white line, it is better to use a scrive, or hollow V-shaped tool which will cut the line at one go.   Semi-circular hollow tools called gouges are used for cutting out white spaces.

Paper.   Each engraver must decide this for himself by experience, discovering what paper suits his particular type of work.   Any good Japanese or India paper will do.   All that is necessary is that for hand printing it should not be too thick to allow of the pressure taking up the ink.

Ink.   This can be any good printing ink, and is best bought in tubes so that it shall not coat or dry.   Coloured inks can be got.   For surface printing avoid any thin ink that will run into the engraved lines and clog them.

In addition to these things a sandbag is needed.   This is a round, flat leather bag filled solidly with sand, and is used as a rest for the wood block.   A rubber roller is required for inking—any photographic one will do ;   a piece of glass or, preferably, a lithographic stone on which to roll the ink, and an ordinary tea spoon for rubbing the print.   For sharpening the tools it is good to have a hard Arkansas stone.

8

THE ARTIST AT WORK

A general view of the artist at work. The block is on the leather sandbag, so that it can be rotated at any moment. The tools are handy at the right side of the wood block, with the handles towards the engraver. It is better to sit with the light towards the left, as the shadows do not then fall on to the lines that are being engraved. Notice the way the little finger is gripped round the handle of the tool.

Method of working. There are various ways of starting, but as the surface of the block is highly polished, it is desirable to cover it with something in order that the tool may not slip. The methods are very individual, determined by whether the artist feels happier evolving the engraving directly out of the wood as he works, letting himself be dictated to more or less by his medium, or whether he wishes to be sure of his design before he starts. For the first, it is better to blacken the block with a coat of Indian ink or black water-colour paint. The design can then be traced on with a red or blue carbon paper, drawn on with a lead pencil that will show shiny, or even engraved direct on to the wood with the tools. Probably this is the highest form, but it pre-supposes great sureness, as it is impossible to erase an engraved line. The second and more usual method is to cover the block with a thin coat of Chinese white. The design can then be drawn or traced with a pencil, carbon paper or black paint. Indian ink should not be used as it is apt to peel off. Care should be taken to " fix " this design on to the wood with an ordinary sprayer and fixatif. Some artists have their drawings photographed on to the block, but this is apt to deaden the work.

The block is now placed on the sandbag. This allows the left hand to grip the sides of the block, and also enables the engraver to swing the block round when a curved line is being cut, for it is the block and not the tool that moves.

The way to hold the tool is best shown by the two photographs on the page opposite. If an even steady line is required, the tool must be held with its point parallel with the surface of the block ; otherwise, if pressed down, it will sink too deep into the wood, or if held too high, will slip up above it. Variety of line is got by variety of depth of cut, for the lower into the wood the tool goes, the bigger is the mark made by the tool, which widens up from its point.

All wood-*engraving* is done *away* from the body.

All wood-*cutting* with a knife is done *towards* the body. There is no rule as to how next to proceed. That must be left to the artist. Some will engrave the main outlines of the design and then take a print, playing about on the

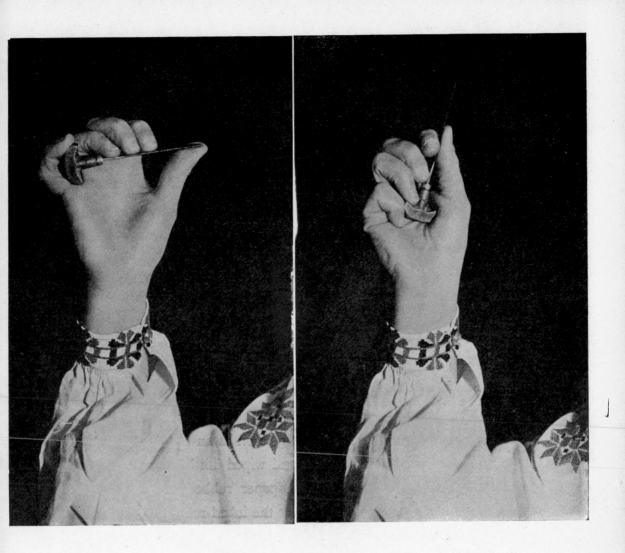

THE WAY TO HOLD THE TOOLS

Left—the right way to hold the tool.   It can then be slid along the edge of the thumb, piston-like, as a line is being engraved.   The head of the tool lodges comfortably in the pad of the palm by the little finger.

Right—an alternative way to hold the tool.   Greater grip is possible this way, but much less freedom of movement from the wrist.   As the engraving of a block is not a matter of sheer physical strength, this way is not really so satisfactory as that illustrated on the left.

rough print with Chinese white in order to see what effect they wish to produce. Some will first remove the wood from the spaces that are to be the large masses of white (this can be done with a gouge or with a chisel and mallet). Others engrave most of the block before taking a print (see Eric Gill, page 25), stopping short only in order to be more certain of the grey values and to clear away any remaining upstanding wood that will catch the ink on the cut away surfaces. Others again (such as Agnes Miller Parker, pages 40 and 45, and J. J. A. Murphy, page 63), take nothing before the final print. This, of course, is easier where the block has been coated with black rather than with white ; powdered French chalk rubbed into the engraved block so entirely gives the effect of the printed block that the actual trial proofing is unnecessary.

Printing. The printing of a block should be as much part of the artist's work as the actual engraving. A detailed account of how this is done will be found under the photographs of the different stages of the process. A block should be so well engraved that it will stand the test of being printed as mechanically as a copper plate visiting card ; on the other hand, provided the particular block is not to be used for book illustration, I see no reason why the artist should not experiment with his printing, even as an etcher is allowed to do. Gauguin lowered parts of his blocks and wiped ink off parts in order to get some of his blacks greyed. Fine sandpaper rubbed over any part of the surface of the block will lower it so that the inked roller does not touch it so strongly—or the ink can be carefully wiped off any desired portion. But care should be taken that none of this amounts to trickery. No individualness of printing should ever be used to hide bad drawing or sloppy, careless engraving.

Particulars of the sharpening of the tools will be found beneath the photograph of this operation (page 21).

Repairs. Any large gash or slip is best repaired by sending the block back to the maker and getting a patch put in. A small slip, however, can be mended by inserting a plug. Drill a hole over the " accident " ; cut and round a tapering peg from a piece of spare boxwood about the size of the drilled hole. Dust the hole with powdered resin, place the peg in the hole and hammer it

TOOL ENGRAVING ON THE BLOCK

Close-up of tool engraving on the block. The wood block is on the sandbag so that the left hand can grip it at the side. The tool is pushed forward by the little finger, and any curve of line is produced by swinging the actual block round. The block in this photograph has already had a trial proof taken of it so that the engraved lines look dark from the cleaning (the petrol-diluted ink has run into them). Note the part of the block that has been scorped out and shows white.

INKING THE ROLLER

The roller is flattening out the sticky black proofing ink on the lithographic stone. (A piece of glass will serve as well, but is apt to get broken or to tear the rubber of the roller if it goes over the edge of the glass.)   This has to be done until the ink on the stone and on the rubber roller is smooth as satin.

INKING THE WOOD BLOCK

The roller charged with this satin-smooth ink is passed over the wood block. Experience alone will determine exactly how much ink to have on the roller. It must be put on very evenly, and it is advisable, before printing, to stand the block up on its four sides and wipe off any ink that may have gone over the edges. This will ensure a perfectly clean outline to the print.

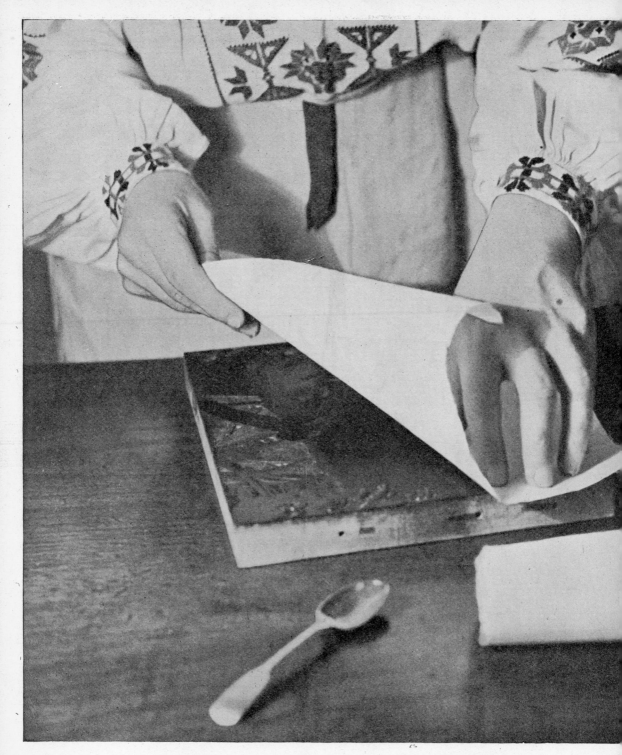

PLACING PRINTING PAPER OVER BLOCK

A piece of printing paper having been cut into the required size—allowing a fair margin all round the block—it is preferably breathed upon, or even damped over the steam from a boiling kettle. This, though, is not necessary. It is then carefully placed over the inked block, care being taken that it should not slip at all. Once placed completely on the block, it is rubbed all over with the palm of the hand to ensure its adhering.

PRINTING THE BLOCK

The actual printing now starts. An ordinary tea spoon is better than any of the burnishers sold, as a greater intimacy is possible. By placing the two first fingers inside the spoon one can feel how one is progressing and can exercise the necessary care over delicate portions of the block. It is better to have a thin smooth card between the spoon and the printing paper as this prevents the spoon from suddenly ripping up the paper. Some people rub a beeswaxed card over the paper to get a smoother surface for rubbing ; but this is not necessary. The entire block should have a general rub so that the eye can see which parts of the block correspond to the printing paper. (N.B.—In this photograph the paper has not been properly pressed down at the left-hand corner. This shows the risk that arises of letting it slip.) The photograph shows by the different colour of it which half of the block has been rubbed and which hasn't. As soon as the general rubbing is finished, the card can be dispensed with and the spoon used in direct touch with the paper. This is so that the black parts can get the extra pressure in order to make them as rich as possible. Care should be taken not to rub hard upon the cut-away white parts. Especial care is needed for the edges of these white parts, else the paper might tear.

C

well in. Part of the peg will be standing above the surface of the block. Take a piece of card, cut a hole in it and slip over the standing part of the peg so that it lies on the surface of the block. Now with a very fine toothed saw cut all round the base of the peg, the block being protected by the card. Any part of the peg remaining above the surface of the block can be shaved with the flat tool and then rubbed with the finest possible sandpaper. Any line which has become bruised by being accidentally pressed down by the back of the tool can be raised by first wetting it and then immediately drying it with a lighted match.

It is not possible to give much in the way of preliminary advice. The only thing to remember is always to be as direct as possible. A re-engraved or touched-up line invariably shows and looks tired. Discover what marks can be made by each tool, make your cut once for all, and get tools of varying thicknesses rather than " go over " any cut that has been made. The best engravings are those in which the tool marks show deliberately.

In the following examples I have chosen prints rather as illustrations of varieties of technique than for their interest as works of art. Careful study of these prints through a magnifying glass will give more help than any amount of reading.

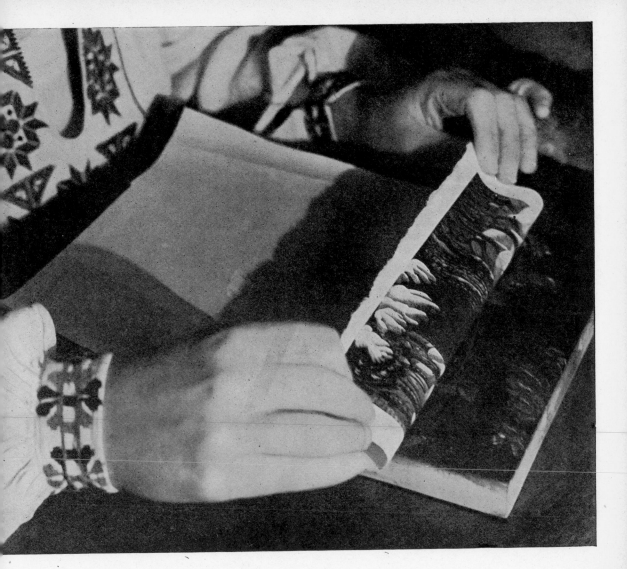

REMOVING PRINT FROM BLOCK

Having rubbed intelligently and discriminately over the surface of the paper, the printer can now dare to lift the paper up from the block. If it is done carefully, practically the entire surface of the print can be looked at before the paper is finally removed ; the only thing to see to is that each part of the paper that has been lifted should be replaced on the block before any other part is raised. This prevents slipping. When it has been ascertained that the print is satisfactory, the paper can be peeled off, as shown in the photograph. This is the finished print.

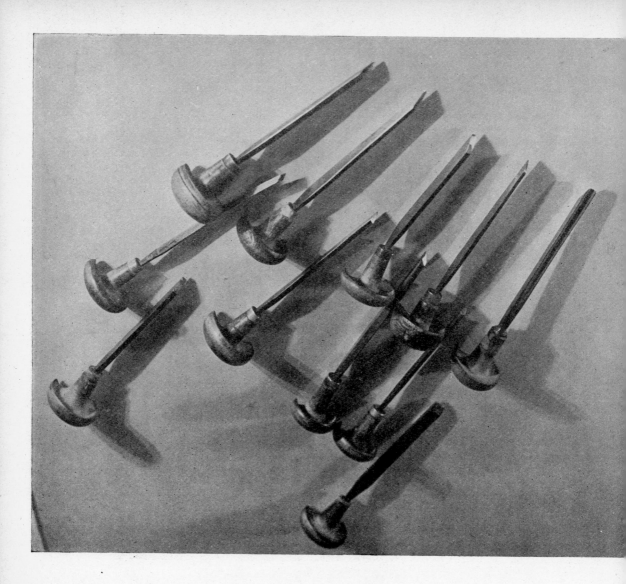

SET OF WOOD-ENGRAVING TOOLS

Top row—left to right :
    1. Rounded scorper. 2. Smaller sized rounded scorper. 3. Square scorper. 4. Smaller square scorper. 5. Gouge for soft wood-cutting.

Second row—left to right :
    1. Graver. 2. Spitzsticker. 3. Large tint tool. 4. Smaller tint tool.

Third row :
    Left : Multiple tool (this does not show clearly, but it is a cross between a square scorper and a rake).
    Right : Flat chisel tool.

It will be noticed that the handles are only rounded at one side so that they may not knock against the block. The slight angle at which the shaft of the tool is fixed into the handle is also shown here.

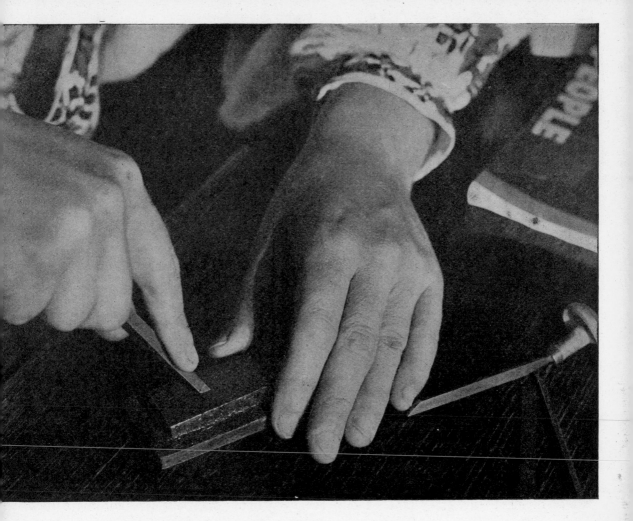

SHARPENING TOOLS

This is a close-up photograph of the sharpening of a tool. Put a few drops of sperm oil or typewriter oil on to a Hard Arkansas oil stone. Grip the handle of the tool in the palm of the right hand with the lower spine of the tool to the front. Place the oblique base of the tool perfectly flat on to the stone in the pool of oil. The greatest care must be taken that it is absolutely flat, else the tool will be sharpened unevenly and the point may be blunted. Move the tool backwards and forwards, up and down or round and round. The direction does not matter so long as the tool keeps flat on the stone. This should sharpen it in a very short while. Try the point across a finger nail and if it sticks into it the tool is sharp enough.

For snapped points or badly blunted tools, a larger, coarser stone may be necessary ; but if the tools are carefully handled they should never get beyond the need for the Hard Arkansas stone.

Remember that a blunt tool means bad work and slipping and mistakes.

21

TOOLS

I. *SCORPERS* (round). Various sizes. The increasing width of the white marks being due to the extra depth that the tool has cut into the wood (that is, that the tool is wider as it goes in deeper). The little jabs and specks on the left are caused by pecking at the wood with the scorper.

II. *GRAVER* (lozenge-shaped). (There is a square one that makes the mark a bit thicker.) The same tool has been used for all these marks, to show the possible variety—all due to the depth of the tool in the wood. This can be seen in the three long lines to the left; pressure has been put in the different parts of the lines and, in the bottom line the pressure has been even throughout. Note the right angle made with the tool.

III. *SPITZSTICKER*. All the marks on this line have also been made with the one-sized tool. The tool, which has oval sides, is the best one always for any curved lines.

IV. *TINT TOOL*. There are very many different sizes of these tools. They have very much less width as they go up the depth of the tool and so are admirable for any work which consists of even white lines. They can be used for straight lines or curved ones. The two tools here shown are of the very fine and the very wide size.

V. *SQUARE SCORPERS*. These shown are of two sizes. They are especially useful for white corners or for lettering.

VI. *FLAT CHISEL*. This tool is used for levelling off the rough cut away parts of large white spaces, so that no upstanding peak of wood may catch the inked roller. It is also good for planing away any edge of a block that is not wanted. An amusing little wriggly mark can (as shown here) be made with it.

22

VII. *MULTIPLE TOOL.* There are two sizes of this tool. It should be used very sparingly and should be avoided altogether until one can manage without it ! It is apt to enslave the artist, as it gives a clever effect with very little trouble. When cross-hatched it gives an effect of a white check pattern on a minute scale.

Print of block cut to show marks made by the different tools.

Wood-engraving tools, blocks and other requisites may be obtained in London from Cornelissen & Sons, T. N. Lawrence, W. Lawrence, Lechertier Barbe Ltd., W. Y. Rhind and C. Roberson & Co. ; in New York through E. H. and A. C. Friedrichs Art Stores, J. Johnson & Co. and Edward C. Muller ; in Chicago through Sandberg & Co. Paper can be obtained in New York through the Stevens-Nelson Paper Co.

ERIC GILL
Self-portrait (First Stage)
(Actual size of print)

We have been especially fortunate in getting the first stage of this *Self-Portrait* by Eric Gill. By comparing this print with the one on the following page, more can be learnt than by reading volumes. Here it will be seen that Eric Gill has engraved everything about which he was certain, not bothering to wait before taking the trial proof until he had cleaned away all the white background. Upstanding bits of wood that have not been removed from the cap and the neck and the forehead still catch the inked roller and print black. The mere position and direction of hair are shown on the beard and eyebrow, and the shadow down the neck, which is grey in the following print, is here still a black space. Compare the weight of the modelling on the face at this stage with the final form. Here the grey under the cheekbone is very obviously crossed white lines on black ; in the next print these white lines will have been crossed so many times more that mere tiny specks of wood will remain to take the ink and print black.

By courtesy of Douglas Cleverdon

Eric Gill. Self-portrait

(First stage. Actual size of print)

By courtesy of Douglas Cleverdon

ERIC GILL
Self-portrait (Final Stage)
(*Actual size of print*)

Here we have the final print. All the background has been cleared away, and the cap and the neck and the shoulder print white. The shadow against the cap and the back of the neck have been greyed by lines engraved across the existing white lines, giving a mesh-like appearance. Notice the work on the hair and the beard, and the fine line where the cap meets the forehead. The modelling on the face has been reduced and extensively lightened. All the odd pieces of upstanding wood have been cleared away, leaving the entire print clean.

So much can be learnt even by taking some small portion—say, the nose—and very carefully studying the difference between this and the first stage.

There is a separate version of this *Self-Portrait* in which large patches have been put into the block behind the ear and above the glasses, bringing the hair up to the ear behind and up to the cap in front.

By courtesy of Douglas Cleverdon

Eric Gill.   Self-portrait

(Final stage.   Actual size of print)
By courtesy of Douglas Cleverdon

In this print the main structure of the design is fixed, but that is about all. Even the horse's head and the cart wheel on the right have only been suggested in pencil upon the first pull. It will be seen that there is a great deal of work in white paint upon this proof, because it was pulled at such an early stage. White paint shows the position of the birdcage and the light on the bundle that is held in the man's hand. It is also used to show where the background on the top left is to be gradually merged at the edges, and to show the modelling of the bundle in the left foreground.

28

THE BIRDCAGE—STAGES I & II

Here the horse's head and the right wheel of the cart have been drawn in, the background at the top left and the man's head and arm engraved. The background at the top left and the horse's head, though, are still too dark to show the required recession, and there is not yet enough light on the man's figure. Also, there is as yet no engraving on the cartwheel. Everything is placed in this stage, but the values are not yet stated.

STAGE II

STAGE III

Here the design required that the light on the bundle in the left foreground should come o~~w~~
solid white, broken even into the border of the print. The top left background has been greye~~d~~
though even now insufficiently. The light has been engraved on the bundle in the cart and the~~r~~
is much more light on the man's figure, to give it solidity. The light parts on the woman's dre~~ss~~
have been whitened and the birdcage has been engraved.

THE BIRDCAGE—STAGES III & IV

Here, in this final stage will be seen the extent to which the entire block has been lightened. Note the white upon the birdcage and the lightening of the horse's head and the wheel, which send these objects into the background. The top left background has been lightened still more at the edges, so that it fades into the white surface in a series of minute black dots and specks, left after much cross-hatching. In this final stage all the values are right and contribute to the design that was aimed at. There is in this print now, too, the sense of solidity in pattern that was lacking in the earlier stages.

STAGE IV

STANISLAW OSTOJA-CHROSTOWSKI
The Wood

This Polish engraving is an interesting contrast to Mrs. Raverat's print. Both show the foliage of trees, but here there is a greater sense of the dramatic and a far wider range of tool work and contrast of tones. Note the strong wide direct cuts upon the near tree trunk at the base against the smooth greys of the background behind the tree ; also, the wiggly black lines at the top right-hand corner.

GWENDOLEN RAVERAT
Bowl Players in France
(Actual size of print)

In Mrs. Raverat's *Bowl Players in France* we have the painter's attitude towards the block rather than the draughtsman's. There is a complete absence of any continuous black or white line outline, the lighted planes on the figures running uninterruptedly into the lighted parts of the background. The texture of the trees is got by a series of pecks with the spitzsticker. The blacks are nearly all greyed by small white lines following the form. The light on the figure with his back towards us is got by cross-hatching white lines running into the scorped-away white part. There is nowhere any direct meeting of black with white.

E

MAURICE DE VLAMINCK
Woodcut
(Greatly reduced)

This large woodcut is the work of a painter rather than of a draughts-man ; but how completely different it is, all the same, from Mrs. Raverat's engraving on the previous page. There is none of her concern with the play of light. Vlaminck has no interest in precision of engraving tech-nique. All he wishes to do is to produce a strong design. Cut with but one tool, and that a large one, he seems to have had little interest, either, in richness of tone values. Contrast the roughly cut edges of the bound-ing border with the cleanness of the Nason print on page 51, to see what wide range this medium of wood gives to the artist, for there is an aliveness in this print that exceeds that in the work of most of the more careful artists, and a richness of quality even in the unvarying tool marks of the print.

MAURICE DE VLAMINCK   Woodcut   Greatly reduced

35

Reduced

MICHAEL PIKOV

The Actress M. Babanova in the play " Profitable Place "

The modern Russian engravers get a silvery quality into their work which is almost unknown in that of the artists of any other country. Favorsky and Kravchenko have this quality, and in this print by Pikov it is very noticeable. The sensitive graver lines follow the form of the surface they wish to create, giving instinctive emphasis to show a swelling of the form, till the regular lines take on almost a feel of steel engraving. Notice this silvery, metallic quality in the work on the woman's dress. The engraved lines are so well controlled that they leave the finest of black lines, so that it is almost like a fine black line drawing rather than an engraving of white upon black. This is one of the best controlled pieces of tool work in existence. Note the precision of the greys of the background, or of the work upon the sleeve. Note too, the fine black lines of the features of the face. Artists of the U.S.S.R. stand high in the world of modern wood-engraving.

36

ERIC GILL
Girl with Cloak
(Actual size of prints)

Eric Gill has printed this block, *Girl with Cloak*, in two ways—(a) surface printing and (b) intaglio. In the intaglio print the ink has been rubbed into the engraved lines and wiped off from the surface of the block. This is the same principle as in etching, and is very rarely used with the wood block. Greater pressure is needed in the printing, which must be done on a press, and the paper must be damped.

JOHN NASH
Pigs

John Nash here has delighted in the wielding of the engraving tool, so that he has allowed himself to be directed by what his tools can do with him. This is evident in the spontaneous tool work of the thatched edge of the top of the pig-sty, and in the engraved lines that curve around the great body of the nearest pig. There is everywhere such delight in his medium. Notice the work in the ground on the left, where he has allowed his tool to take him where and as it would. And with it all, there is a great range of tone values, from the rich black of the right foreground through the many greys to the white of the sunlit fence. Never does he make two marks with a tool where one will do.

ROCKWELL KENT
The End

This is one of the best of the many engravings of Rockwell Kent. Some of his prints have developed almost a formula of technique, but here there is rich variety which gives a strong sense of form to his design. Look carefully at the form of the nearest wave, with its rich white and turned-over edge, and compare it with the treatment of the water pouring into the back of the little boat. Notice, too, the sense of depth given to the water in the tiny specks of white made by the tint tool as the greys of the waves merge into the black of the water. Notice, too, the strength of the white in the sky, emphasized by contrast with the greys and the blacks.

AGNES MILLER PARKER
Fox and Raysyns

This artist is probably one of the most highly skilled engravers living—outside of the old school of professional non-creative artist engravers. No one can equal her in her delicate merging of blacks into whites through infinite varyings of greys. Take note of the countless fine white lines made with the tint tool and white specks made by a small scorper that form these greys, and the reader will see the extent of her amazing craftsmanship. Notice also the cleanness of her outlines everywhere and the skill of her treatment of the fox's fur. This print shows the best use that can be made of sensitive cross-hatching. It is a splendid example of modern work, from which much can be learned.

ASA CHEFFETZ   Up North

There is an amazing richness of tone quality in this print. Note the crispness of the work on the loose timber of the barns, how it sparkles. The extreme softness of the treatment of the meadowland with its undulating form is made by uncountable specks of the tint tool in the foreground and the soft tiny round jabs of a minute rounded scorper in the distant grassland. Note, too, the light the artist has got into his sky with the fine parallel lines of the graver that deepen and widen against the silhouetted buildings and mountains. This is a fine print from which to learn about delicate technique. Compare it with the Miller Parker engraving.

F

BLAIR HUGHES-STANTON
The Sons and Daughters

This print by Blair Hughes-Stanton is exceedingly interesting. It is about as clean in its cutting as it is humanly possible for it to be. There is no " bruising " in any of the fine white line drawing, and no " spluttering " in any of the curves.

Notice the extremely fine engraving of the greys upon the thin drapery ; they are never monotonous, for the treatment varies over the surface of the print, so that in some places they are made by a series of very fine parallel lines and in others by cross-hatching, while yet again the greys are lightened by tiny white specks cut into the cross-hatching.

Notice, too, the way the artist has given a feeling of distance to the clump of flowers between the two feet on the right by greying it over and above the actual work on the flowers and the ground themselves. There is such variety in the rich treatment of the ground that much could be learnt—both here and over most of the print—by looking at it through a magnifying glass. Blair Hughes-Stanton, Agnes Miller Parker and Gertrude Hermes are the three engravers who have perhaps, of all others, combined a modern creative vision with amazingly fine technique.

43

l'avantage soit pour toi, laisse-lui l'honneur : tu ne perdras
rien à lui donner le rôle d'une personne toute-puissante
[sur ton esprit]. Mais, si tu as à cœur de conserver l'amour
de ton amie, fais en sorte qu'elle te croie émerveillé de sa
beauté. Porte-t-elle un manteau en pourpre de Tyr ? Vante
les manteaux en pourpre de Tyr. Porte-t-elle un tissu de Cos ?
Pense que le tissu de Cos lui va bien. Est-elle brillante d'or ?
Dis-lui qu'à tes yeux elle a plus de prix que l'or. Si elle a
choisi une étoffe épaisse, loue l'étoffe qu'elle a choisie. Si elle
t'apparaît vêtue de la seule tunique, crie : "Tu m'embrases";
mais timidement prie-la de se garantir du froid. Elle est
coiffée en bandeaux simples ? Vante les bandeaux. Le fer
a-t-il bouclé ses cheveux ? Cheveux bouclés, il faut que vous
plaisiez. Admire ses bras, quand elle danse, sa voix, quand
elle chante, et, dès qu'elle cesse, plains-toi qu'elle ait fini.
Vos embrassements mêmes et ce qui fait ton bonheur, tu
pourras les célébrer et les voluptés secrètes qu'elle goûte
la nuit. Fût-elle plus farouche que l'effrayante Méduse,
elle deviendra douce et bienveillante pour son soupirant.

ARISTIDE MAILLOL

This page from a fine French edition of Ovid's " Art of Love," with a decoration by
the sculptor Maillol, is an exquisite example of the unity attainable between letterpress
and illustration. The weight of the type and the weight of the outlines of the figures
is a perfect balance. Typography by P. Gouin, Paris. Published in Gt. Britain by
A. Zwemmer. Size 15 × 11 in.

THE FABLES OF
ESOPE

TRANSLATED OUT OF FRENSSHE IN TO
ENGLYSSHE BY: WILLIAM CAXTON

WITH ENGRAVINGS ON WOOD BY AGNES MILLER PARKER

THE GREGYNOG PRESS: NEWTOWN
MONTGOMERYSHIRE: - MCMXXXI

AGNES MILLER PARKER

Title page by William McCance for the Gregynog Press " *Fables of Esope,*" with decoration by Agnes Miller Parker and lettering cut by William McCance. This is a splendid example of a well-designed title page, letterpress and engraving blending into a most harmonious whole. The balance is obtained by the general colour of the print instead of by the weight of the line, as was shown in the example on the opposite page. Size 12 × 8½ in.

GERTRUDE HERMES
Autumn Fruits
(13½ *in. wide*)

From the technical point of view this print might almost be called a sample page of possible tool marks for there is rich variety, from the different sized scorpers to the finest lines made with the tint tool. And not only is there variety of tool, but variety in the use of each tool, so that sometimes the scorper will make a long curving line and sometimes a mere jab of white. It is all of it completely spontaneous work, done with the utmost deliberation. The strength of cut in some of the places gives real contrast to the fine greys in others.

Notice the solidity the artist has been able to get into the form of the mushrooms. There is countless variety in the greys, and here they are simple fine lines, there they are reinforced with white specks. One characteristic of Gertrude Hermes' work is the way she will cut a strong white line upon the already engraved grey, as in part of the underside of the mushroom on the right.

The feeling for form and texture has excited the artist so much that she has no rule as to how she should model her objects. She obeys her instinct, and it is invariably a sure one.

This print is a mine of information.

GERTRUDE HERMES

Autumn Fruits

Courtesy of the Redfern Gallery, London

47

DEMETRIUS GALANIS
The Three Graces

This print shows better than any the good and purposeful use of the multiple tool. There is a rich moulding of the nude figures that could hardly have been produced by any other means. Except for the small piece of drapery in the bottom left-hand corner, there is no use made of any other tool. This concentration on the multiple tool gives an atmosphere of sophistication that entirely suits the subject. It is essentially a Gallic work of art.

The multiple tool has been used almost as though it were a paint brush and the figures are modelled in a plastic manner rather than with the eye of the calligraphic draughtsman.

There is a very subtle sense of distance in the fragment of suggested landscape behind the tree trunk on the left.

It is especially interesting to note the amazing number of varying greys that Galanis has produced with this one tool, contrasting his little thin white lines again and again until he can reach a pure white for his highlights.

Courtesy of the Whitworth Art Gallery, Manchester

G

49

KÄTHE KOLLWITZ
Self-portrait

    This woodcut is an example of the work of the modern German school which was interested in vibrant designs of black and white rather than in any fineness of delicate technique. Sensitive, exquisite draughtsman that she is, Käthe Kollwitz abandons herself to the excitement of the moment of creating, and with rough, crude cuts produces a head that is solid in bulk and true in form. Note the grey tone on the chin and the cheek to the left, where either the surface of the block was lowered or the ink partially wiped off.

T. W. NASON
Silo and Barn

In strong contrast to the forceful power and rough cutting of the German woodcut shown on the opposite page, this delicate print of T. W. Nason's looks doubly fine. There is a serenity about this work that is most beautiful. Note the extreme cleanness of the engraving and the subtle variation of greys that is produced by slightly thicker or thinner lines engraved. Note also that, unlike many engravers, Nason does not outline his objects with white, but lets them fall against or stand out from each other by a tone of black. This is some of the most lyrical work being produced to-day in America.

These three small engravings are examples of how suitable the wood block is for decorating the printed book.

Clare Leighton's *Mice* and Ethelbert White's *illustration from "Walden"* were both engraved for the Penguin Books, Ltd., to be sold

1. PETER STARONOSSOV
Illustration to a children's book

2. ETHELBERT WHITE
Illustration from Thoreau's "Walden"

3. CLARE LEIGHTON
Mice

very inexpensively indeed. These, as also is the case with most of the modern Soviet wood-engravings, go to prove the advantage of using the wood block for cheap reproduction —it will print clearly and well on quite ordinary paper and stands up to a large run of printing.

K. WISZNIEWSKI

St. Christopher

($7\frac{7}{8} \times 7\frac{1}{2}$ in.)

This print shows the interesting quality that can be got by uneven cutting at the edges of the white spaces, which gives a speckled roughness. There is no striving after any greys or subtleties. The artist has designed in the two simple tones of black and white. It is a grand example of balance of design.

53

J. ROULLET
The Church at Vomécourt in Lorraine
($12\frac{7}{8} \times 15\frac{7}{8}$ *in.*)

This is a typically French print, with all the grace that one associates with the work of France. The original engraving is a very large one, but in this unavoidable reduction we can yet see the variety of the engraving. The artist was more interested in tone values than in any actual drawing and nowhere do we see any significant lines such as there are in John Nash's print *Foxgloves* on the opposite page.

From " Poisonous Plants " (Haselwood Press)

JOHN NASH   Foxgloves   *(Actual size of print)*

There is great range of tool work in this study of *Foxgloves* by John Nash. Most of the cutting has been done by different sized scorpers, though the engraving on the flowers in the top left-hand corner has been done with the graver. John Nash is never afraid to show the marks of his tools.

55

Decoration (*Courtesy of The Goupil Gallery*)

ERIC GILL
Page from " The Canterbury Tales "
(*Actual size*)

Eric Gill has here, in this page from Chaucer's *Canterbury Tales*, shown us an engraving successfully married to type, the weight of line being in each case about equal. The whole principle of this block is one of black lines on white, which involves the double work of cutting away the surface of the wood on either side of the remaining upstanding black line. The actual scorper marks are shown on the scallops under the bed, and the shading of the leaves is made by scorping from the central veins outwards, so that the instinctive additional pressure on the tool towards the end of the cut thins the remaining black lines towards the outside. The large areas of white may in a case like this be removed mechanically. This print is an answer to those people who complain that a wood-engraving is *always* too black properly to balance the weight of the type, and so should not be used as a book illustration.

Disposeth ay your hertes to withstonde
The feend, that yow wolde make thral and bonde.
He may nat tempten yow over your might;
For Crist wol be your champion and knight.
And prayeth that thise Somnours hem repente
Of hir misdedes, er that the feend hem hente.

T HIS Somnour in his stiropes hye stood;
Upon this Frere his herte was so wood,
That lyk an aspen leef he quook for yre.
'Lordinges,' quod he, 'but o thing I desyre;
I yow biseke that, of your curteisye,
Sin ye han herd this false Frere lye,
As suffereth me I may my tale telle!
This Frere bosteth that he knoweth helle,
And god it woot, that it is litel wonder;
Freres and feendes been but lyte asonder.
For pardee, ye han ofte tyme herd telle,
How that a frere ravisshed was to helle
In spirit ones by a visioun;
And as an angel ladde him up and doun,

91

C. W. TAYLOR
East Anglia
$(12\frac{1}{4} \times 10 \; in.)$

This print by C. W. Taylor shows absolutely the opposite approach to that of Eric Gill's on the previous page. Here the entire work has been white upon black. There is not much variety of tool work, the direction of the white line being used to denote the planes. There is very little use of any large spaces of pure white except in the cleared sky. It is as though the artist's main concern were with the play of light, and with this use always of white line upon black, he achieves his purpose with astonishing success, so that in all his prints there is the sense of the flooding of sunlight.

Note the direct tool marks by means of which he shows the foliage on the trees: long thin marks with the spitzsticker on the nearer tree, short broad marks with the graver on the far one. Note also the way in which he gets the uneven surface of the lane by means of the direction of his white lines.

(*Design for an L.N.E.R. poster*)

C.W.TAYLOR

59

TIMOTHY COLE
Abraham Lincoln
($11 \times 8\frac{1}{2}$ *in.*)

The American master-engraver, Timothy Cole, here shows us the tone possibilities in a wood-engraving. This amazing piece of craftsmanship is about the high water mark in its own line. Spiritually, it belongs to the middle of the last century, and Timothy Cole quite frankly admits to working from a photograph on the block. But it is an astonishing feat. Note the interesting treatment of grey in the framework ground, made by cutting wide parallel lines one way and then cutting across them more finely, leaving upstanding dots of black. Look very closely into the mesh-like work that gives the grey tone and modelling to the face. The form is got by multitudinous cross-hatched curving parallel lines, a wider tool being used where, as on the nose and the cheekbone, a whiter light is needed. Unlike some of the moderns, Timothy Cole never cross-hatches his lines more than once.

By courtesy of William Edwin Rudge, New York

Timothy Cole 1928

61

J. J. A. MURPHY
The Four Horsemen of the Apocalypse
($11\frac{3}{4} \times 11\frac{1}{4}$ *in.*)

I have purposely put *The Four Horsemen of the Apocalypse*, by J. J. A. Murphy, directly following Timothy Cole's *Abraham Lincoln*, as it makes a most interesting extreme. The one artist was intent on copying tone and the other on creating form ; each being a fine craftsman in his own way. J. J. A. Murphy prepares his design on his block very carefully with black and white paint, knowing beforehand exactly what his greys are to be and on which planes. He then engraves the entire block without taking a trial proof, using an exceedingly large number of tools so that he knows which size scorper is needed for which particular grey. By cutting the block up into these over-emphasized planes a great feeling of strength is given.

Notice the extreme cleanness of the cutting. There are no fine lines in this print, but the range of cutting is so large that it makes some lines look fine by comparison.

Insufficiently known in his own country, this American wood-engraver produces engravings of outstanding vitality and beauty.

This is a print to learn much from, for the craftsman as well as for the artist.

J. J. A. MURPHY

The Four Horsemen of the Apocalypse

SAKHNORSKAYA
Woman in the 1905 Revolution

This print from Soviet Russia has the crispness that we associate with wood-engravings from that country. In places it is almost like a pen and ink drawing of black upon white, for example—in the work on the front of some of the dresses or the central man's apron. This black upon white work is a tremendous *tour de force*, for it means the most precise cutting up against the remaining lines.

There is a strength and an aliveness about this Soviet school of modern wood-engraving that is unequalled—whereas the English allow themselves to be perhaps too much dominated by craftsmanship, and the Germans have little concern for it, concentrating upon the emotion of their subject. The Russians seem able to combine the good executive development with an aliveness that the English lack. They are especially inclined to be less constrained in the shape of the borders of their prints, and use the outside of the page as part of the actual design.

1905
1905

I

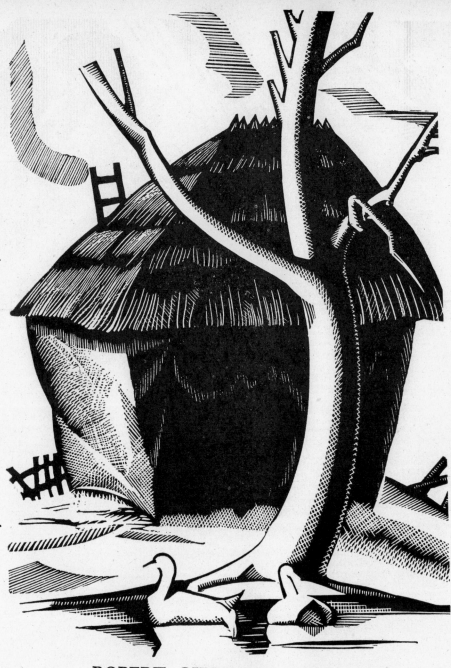

ROBERT GIBBINGS   Bloggs Pond

This is an outstandingly good example of the contribution that Mr. Gibbings has made to modern wood-engraving. His design is reduced to the simplest terms and he is content to create his forms by three tones—sheer black, absolute white and a merging grey composed of uncomplicated cross-hatchings of white lines. This is seen here to best advantage in his treatment of the tree trunk. His work has exceptional cleanness of cutting. He always prints his engravings well and his blacks have an outstanding richness of quality.

PAUL NASH
Promenade

Interested most in using wood-engraving as a means of making solid, three dimensional designs, Paul Nash does not concern himself much with the actual tool work of an engraving. He controls his tools rather than delights in what they can do *with* him, so that there is an intellectual quality about his prints that does not bother about any actual beauty of engraved line. But look at this print from some distance away, and you will see that it has a singing quality of tone and an amazing strength of plane—apart from the beauty of its actual design as it covers the paper. In its distribution of blacks and whites and greys it is outstanding, and it is a thing apart from the work of Gill, Raverat, Parker or Hughes-Stanton. There is an aliveness about it that often is lacking in the usual work of the school of modern English print makers, who interest themselves perhaps unduly much with the actual technique.

PAUL LANDACRE
Storm

$(8 \times 10\frac{1}{8}\ in.)$

    Paul Landacre is outstandingly successful in his feeling for light. And to get that light he always leaves a full balance of deep black and grades his white with his black by cross-hatched and fine white lines.

    He has made an interesting use of the superimposing of thicker white marks upon the greyed surface of the water.

    This is the print of an artist who knows that he can get what he wants from the wood block.

DAVID JONES
Everyman

David Jones is another modern-minded artist who expresses himself in wood-engraving. He has a very subjective attitude towards his block and, while not thinking as consciously as most artists about the technique of his medium, achieves some extraordinary qualities. There is a tapestry-like feeling in his design. By separating and outlining his forms in white he gets a most interesting solidity. Contrasting this print with Paul Landacre's on the opposite page, we note that David Jones rarely leaves any large surface of black—his concern is more with subtlety of design.

IRENE KOLSKY
The Sower

This print has a great deal in common with the modern German school and with such artists as Barlach. There is a rough quality about it, as though the artist were concerned solely with the emotional content of the subject matter. But in spite of this roughness, there yet is an exciting sense of colour, so that the light figure of the sower stands out vibrantly against the grey of the furrowed field. There is, too, a solidity that is most satisfying. Notice the economy of cutting upon the hands and the feet that yet achieves its purpose and gives us some quite beautiful drawing.

71

PAL C. MOLNAR
The Two Dogs
($11\frac{7}{8} \times 9\frac{7}{8}$ *in.*)

There is almost a shiny stickiness about this clever print, due to the facile use of the multiple tool. With what ease the dogs have been engraved, or the bars of the fence or the modelling on the girl's dress ! But apart from this, there is great variety of tool work upon the ground, and interesting modelling upon the face and arms of the girl.

The multiple tool used by this artist is a larger one than usual, so that the whole effect is more vital. Also, the strong masses of white give a sense of values to the greys of the multiple tool work that prevents any monotony.

Birger Sandzen   River Nocturne

BIRGER SANDZEN
River Nocturne
(Reduced reproduction)

In direct contrast is this *River Nocturne*, by Birger Sandzen. This print has been done entirely with the scorper, the whole effect being one almost of wool work or bead work. There are hardly any continuous lines, and all the tool marks seem about the same size. It would be difficult to find a greater difference of outlook than between this print and the one opposite—in spite of the fact that both are landscapes.

ERIC RAVILIOUS
Sussex Landscape

Courtesy of the Redfern Gallery

There is great variety of tool work in this print, so that it is especially interesting to compare it with the Birger Sandzen block on the opposite page which was made with but one tool. Notice the way the rounded hill has been managed, with lines and jabs and specks of many sizes. The same resourcefulness of tool work can be seen in the treatment of the roof of the house.

WLADYSLAW SKOCZYLAS
The Old Mountain Farmer
($14\frac{1}{4} \times 11\frac{3}{4}$ *in.*)

Skoczylas was the father of the rich school of the modern wood block in Poland.   This print, cut on pearwood and worked the way of the grain, inevitably has none of the fineness of craftsmanship to be found in the work of such engravers as Blair Hughes-Stanton or Agnes Miller Parker. Instead, there is a direct, uncompromising force about it that is in keeping with its subject matter.   It is genuine work, and in its rough way completely respectful of its medium.   There is no sign of any consciousness of fashion or sophistication.

Note the rich solid form of the trousers, got by the most direct, unaffected cutting.   Note also the sense of colour, ranging from the white shirt through the tone of the old mountain farmer's face, to the black of his coat.

There is no cross-hatching in this print and never have two cuts been made where one would serve.

ALEXIS KRAVCHENKO
Illustration to *Quiet Don*

There is the same strange silvery quality in this print that is so often found in modern Russian wood-engravings. Kravchenko is one of the leaders of the remarkably fine school of Soviet engravers and book illustrators. The sparkle upon the water in this print is uncanny and though the regularity of the lines in the sky might seem almost mechanical, yet it has an exciting feeling to it. The whole engraving is sensitive and beautiful in colour.

WANDA GAG
Spinning Wheel

By courtesy of The Weyhe Gallery, New York

A technique consisting nearly entirely of little jabs with a small scorper, varied by even smaller jabs with a graver.   Differences of light are got by varying lengths of tool marks, close together or further apart.

Note that there is no continuous white line engraving in this print.   Compare it with the Soviet print on the opposite page.

CLARE LEIGHTON

In this illustration for *Under the Greenwood Tree*, I have tried to combine a sense of calligraphic drawing and design with an interest on tone values. By cutting pure white upon the highlight of the figures and upon the sheaf of wheat in the foreground I have managed to throw the whole landscape into the background.

THE HISTORY OF HERODOTUS

THESE ARE THE RESEARCHES OF HERODOTUS OF HALICARNASSUS WHICH HE PUBLISHES TO PRESERVE FROM DECAY THE REMEMBRANCE OF WHAT MEN HAVE DONE AND TO PREVENT GREAT AND WONDERFUL ACHIEVEMENTS OF BOTH GREEKS AND FOREIGNERS FROM LOSING THEIR GLORY AND ESPECIALLY TO MAKE KNOWN THE CAUSE OF WAR BETWEEN THEM

A passage in Aristotle's Rhetoric (perhaps interpolated by a copyist) quotes the opening sentence with the author's name as «Herodotus of Thurium», and Plutarch knew this form as a variant; all extant manuscripts read «Halicarnassus». Incidentally, Herodotus' use of historia, «research», here and in vii. 95, apparently established the specialised meaning of the word, «history». For a literary and historical consideration of this sentence, see Wilhelm Schmid, Philologische Wochenschrift, 1932, col. 1001.

Page from The Nonesuch Press HERODOTUS (London, 1935). Decoration by V. LE CAMPION (11¼ × 7 in.)

V. LE CAMPION

This page of an edition of *Herodotus*, engraved by V. Le Campion is yet another example of good balance in book illustration. The loosely bordered margin is a perfect blend with the white spaces left between the letters at the top of the page. There is some of the same technique in this Frenchman's work that we find in the engravings of many of the modern Russians—especially in the treatment of the drapery on the seated figure. We must look carefully at the cutting on the subtle piece of landscape beneath the sun. The grey spiral within the sun itself is a *tour de force*.

L

EDWARD GORDON CRAIG
Two Pages from " The Tragedie of Hamlet "
(Reduction to ⅖ of original page size)

This is another interesting example of an individual manner of printing
—this time in book form.   Count Kessler, in his famous *Hamlet*, illustrated by Gordon Craig, has a very beautiful grey tone on his whole page.
Compare the manner of doing this with the page from Eric Gill's *Canterbury Tales* (page 57), where the balance has been got by the black line
engraving being of the same weight as the type.   Here, Craig has cut his
blocks with single white outlines, and the whole tone effect is given by the
printing.   The ink has three degrees of blackness.

By courtesy of The Cranach Press

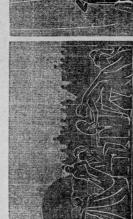

Rue pour
finasse de
Amleth.

Ainsi furent deputez quelques courtisans, pour mener le Prince en quelque lieu escarté, dans le boys, et lesquels luy presentas-sent ceste femme, l'incitans à se souiller en ses bayses et embras-semens, artifices assez frequent

Corruption de la
Ieunesse de
courtisans
grands.

de nostre temps, non pour es-sayer si les grands sont bors de leur sens, mais pour les priver de force, vertu et sagesse, par le moyen de ses satisnes et inter-nalles Lamies, produites par les serviteurs, ministres de corrup-tion. Le pauvr Prince eust cost en danger de succomber à cost assaut si un Gentil-bomme, qui du vivant de Horwendille, avoit este nourry avec luy, ne se fust plus monstre amie de la nourri-ture prinse avec Amleth, que affec-tionne à la puissance du tyran, lequel pour bassoit les moyens de envelopper le fils es pieges, es-quels le pere avoit fny ses jours. Cestuy s'accompagna des courtisans deputez pour ceste tra-hison, plus avec deliberation d'instruire le Prince, de ce qu'il avoit à faire, que pour luy dresser des embusches et le trahir, estimant que le moindre indice qu'il donneroit de son bon sens, suffiroit pour luy faire perdre la vie. Cestuy-cy avec certains signes fair entendre à Amleth, en quel peril est ce qu'il se mettroit, si en sorte aucune il obeissoit aux mignardes caresses, et mignotises de la Damoyselle, envoyee par son oncle, ce qui estonnant le Prince esmeu de la beauté de la fille, fut par elle asseuré encor de la trahison, car elle l'aymoit de son enfance, et eust este marrie de son mal heur, et moins de le voir mourir de la fille, soustenans qu'il ne s'estoit avancé en sorte aucune à la violer, quoy qu'il dict du contraire, chacun s'asseura que veritablement il estoit insense, et que son cerveau n'avoit force quelconque, capable d'apprehension raisonable.

Enter Hamlet, and three of the Players.

Ham. Speake the speech I pray you as I pronounc'd it to you, trippingly on the tongue, but if you mouth it as many of our Players do, I had as live the towne cryer spoke my lines, nor doe not saw the ayre too much with your hand thus, but use all gently, for in the very torrent tem-pest, and as I may say, whirlwind of your pas-sion, you must acquire and beget a temperance, that may give it smoothnesse, O it offends mee to the soule, to heare a robustious perwig-pated fellowe tere a passion to totters, to very rags, to spleet the eares of the groundlings,

60

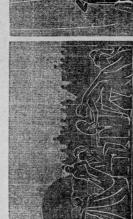

who for the most part are capable of nothing but inexplicable dumbe showes, and noyse, I would have such a fellow whipt for ore-doo-ing Termagant, it out-Herods Herod, pray you avoyde it.

Play. I warrant your honour.
Ham. Be not too tame neither, but let your owne dis-cretion be your tutor, sute the action to the word, the word to the action, with this speciall obser-vance, that you ore-steppe not the modestie of nature: For any thing so ore-doone, is from the purpose of playing, whose end both at the first, and nowe, was and is, to holde as twere

subtilty, such as one day might be preiudiciall to their prince, saying that under colour of such rudenes be shadowed a crafty pollicy, and by his devised sim-plicitye, be concealed a sharp and pregnant spirit, for which cause they counselled the king to trye, knowe if it were possible, howe to discover the intent and meaning of the yong prince, & they could find no better, normore fit invention to intrap him then to set some faire, and beawtifull woman in secret place, that with flattering speeches, and all the craftiest meanes she could use, should purposely seek to allure his minde to have his pleas-ure of her, for the nature of all young men, (specially such as are brought up wantonlie) is so transported with the desires of the flesh, and entreth so greed-ily into the pleasures thereof, that it is almost impossible to cover that foul affliction neither yet to dissemble or byde the same by art or industry, much lesse to shunne it. What cunning or subtilty so ever they use to cloak their pretence, seeing occasion offered, and that in secret, specialty in the most inticing sinne that rayneth in man, they cannot chuse (being constrayned by voluptuousnesse) but fall to naturall effect and working. To this end certaine courtiers were appointed to leade Hamlet into a solitary place within the woods, whether they brought the woman, inciting him to take their pleasures together, and to imbrace one another, but the suttle practises used in those our dayes, not to try if men of great account bee retract out of their strength, to deprive them of strength, vertue, and wisedome, by meanes of such diveilish practitioners, and so consequently the ruine of a vertuous life, the overthrow and mistresse of corruption, and surely the poore prince at this assault had bin in great daner, if a gentle-man (that in Horvendiles time had bin nourished with him) had not showne himselfe more

Nature
corrupted
in man.

Subtiltie used
to discover
Hamlets
madnes.

61

83

PAUL GAUGUIN
Tepo, Goddess of Night

Though he is not of this generation, Gauguin's woodcut is included as a thing of great interest in the widest range of possibility of execution. He was no respecter of his tools. His block and his knife had to obey him. He would cut and scrape on the roughest kind of plank—odd pieces found, after his death, to be stopping up pig-sties in Tahiti. There is a wild vigour in the slashes he makes with his gouge and a great deal of use is made of the grain of the wood. In places the surface of the block is lowered so that it may not receive the full amount of ink. Sometimes the grain is so pronounced and rough that there are long seams which the ink fails to reach.

Sometimes, too, he is supposed to have used some sort of steel wire with which to scratch his fine white lines, while often the crudest of tools served to cut away his whites.

In the printing of his blocks the already uneven ink is wiped off in places so that large spaces of grey may be seen.

STEFAN MROZEWSKI
Design for Don Quixote Series

This is another engraving which, like that on page 49, shows the intelligent use of the multiple tool. But whereas Galanis used practically only this tool, Mrozewski has varied his technique by using quite a variety of tool marks. He has produced a certain sharpness of feeling by the strong straight lines and wide round cuts in the right bottom foreground and in the ground at the top of the picture which contrasts with the silvery feeling of the multiple tool work of the background behind the figure of Don Quixote. Unlike a great many users of this treacherous tool, he has not allowed himself to let his sense of design be obscured.

By retaining strong masses of black, such as in the left foreground and even upon the shield, he has been able fully to exploit the silvery quality of the greys and thus has added force and drama to his design.

NELLY DEGOUY   Le Cercle De Famille

This is an example of sophistication in a print that contrasts with the honest strength of the one on the opposite page.

EDMUND BARTLOMIEJCZYK
Going to Work
$(9\frac{7}{8} \times 12\frac{1}{2}\ in.)$

Going to Work is a most satisfying print, full of integrity as are all the woodcuts produced by the Poles, and in keeping with their tradition of direct, next to the earth healthiness of approach. This artist has been interested more in what he wished to say than in the manner in which he would say it, so that it is a splendid foil to the print opposite.

The engravings on these two
pages are to show that the days
of the professional commercial
engraver are still with us. These,
engraved by a firm in Chicago,
are amazing examples of technical skill. There has been a
great deal of intelligent use of
the multiple tool, to give the
feeling of smooth shine to some
of the metal. The texture of
the cases has been achieved by
subtle criss-cross work with the
multiple tool.

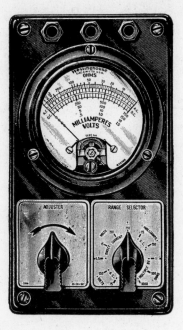

Note the incredible skill of the work on the tiny lettering, which has, of course, to be engraved backwards in order that it may print the right way round. Note, too, the clean sure outlines and the precision of all the curves.

Though these are not the work of creative artists, in that they are merely the use of the wood block for the purpose of reproduction, yet they are such amazingly fine examples of craftsmanship that all creative wood-engravers would do well to study them closely.

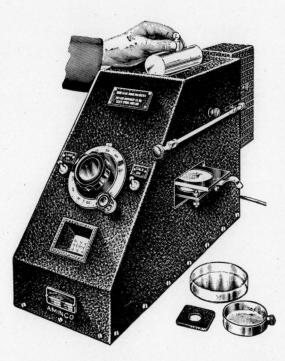

THREE TYPES OF PRINTING

OVER-INKED PRINT

In this print which has been purposely over-inked, it will be seen that the fine white lines on the buildings in the top background have been completely lost under the excess of ink. In the same way the lines on the tree and on the foliage, as well as those on the bottom right side of the ground are smothered in the ink. The glimpse of background of trees is out of all proportion over-black, so that the sense of three dimensions is destroyed. Above all, apart from the loss of the white line engraving all over the block, there is an inevitable feeling of flatness due to the uniform blackness.

Here, on the other hand, there are no dramatic blacks. Everything is pale and under-emphasized. While the white lines show everywhere, they yet do not have the significance that they should have because the range from dead white to deepest black is limited by the under-inking. Although the buildings in the top background are a beautiful silvery grey, yet they do not recede enough from the tree branch and the figure, because nowhere is there a true black.

CORRECTLY INKED PRINT

Here it will be seen that there is a combination of the good points of both of the preceding prints. The top background is still silvery grey and the fine white lines have nowhere been lost through over-inking. But in this case the greys have their full meaning because the kneeling figure is an intense black, so that the full range of colour and tone is achieved.

93

FINALE

When we face the enormous rush of wood-engravings produced nowadays, we ask ourselves what are the reasons for the modern use of this medium as the artist's direct means of expression.

The reasons, I feel, are several and very definite. To start with, there is the unromantic but unavoidable consciousness of economic conditions and demands. A widening of the circle of good taste through the spread of education has brought about a desire for original works of art. But this bigger public is not wealthy. Fortunately, the boxwood block, unlike the copper plate, will yield an almost indefinite number of perfect prints. A large edition of a wood-engraving at a low price is therefore the ideal thing to satisfy the modern public in the modern home. And always, through the centuries, demand has produced and directed supply. In its pioneering days wood-engraving leapt into popularity to meet the need of pilgrims who wanted a souvenir of the shrine they had visited. It was used to decorate the calendars and the manuals of devotion, which were almost the only printed books that had in those days a wide circulation. In our own day it is interesting to note that while the disappearance of a leisured upper class in Russia has all but killed the demand for studio paintings, the growth of a vast new public of readers has brought an immense stimulus to wood-engraving.

In the modern world generally a continually increasing number of illustrated books are concentrating on wood-engravings. Probably one of the main reasons for this is the mechanical ease with which the engravings can be printed on the same paper as the type, whereas illustrations in so many other mediums have to be printed on separate paper and bound in. This understanding of the harmony and balance possible between the wood-engraving and the printed page is best seen in the work of Eric Gill and Maillol. Most artists overbalance the type with too much blackness in the wood block.

94

But the wood-engraving should not limit itself to this ambition. Working for book reproduction is distinctly hampering. The artist must always restrict himself to the required dimensions. Worse still, he must adjust his temperament and outlook too much to the book to be illustrated. Above all, he must only engrave the kind of work that will reproduce mechanically without loss to its quality. Any original effects of printing, too, are impossible when the block has to be handed over to the professional printer, and very fine white lines are apt to get clogged with ink.

Used as a wall picture, the wood-engraving, with its rich design in black and white, is pre-eminently in keeping with modern ideas of interior decoration and harmonises with the primary colours that are being used in houses to-day.

More interesting are the reasons why the artist wants to do wood-engraving. We are more exacting and scientific than our fathers were, and the wood block, through its wider range of keyboard from blackest black to dead white, permits of far greater precision of tone and of a much stronger rendering of form, which is the intellectual element. Compare its possibilities with the relatively restricted range of the etching, where the white is never white and the black at deepest is a dark brown. Fatigued with the photographic representation of life in the more conventional etching, we call for greater subjectiveness. This is more readily attainable in the wood-engraving than in any other medium. These illustrations show the wide variety of technique that can be achieved. The draughtsman, the painter, the sculptor, the decorative designer, the traditional objective artist, and the modern abstract artist, one and all can satisfy their particular special talents and temperaments to a degree impossible in any other medium. Compare the painter's mind of Mrs. Raverat with the sculptor's mind of Eric Gill. Where are there to be found greater extremes than the " *Autumn Fruits* " engraving of Gertrude Hermes, with its subjective outlook, and the calm traditional feeling of C. W. Taylor's *East Anglia* ? Or, again, what difference there is between the informing draughtsmanship of Agnes Miller Parker and the naive creativeness of David Jones.

The wood-engraving appeals to any artist who loves strong, clean, deliberate drawing, for it is impossible on the wood block to " codge " or re-state. The thinking must be done before the engraving, and whereas in the etched plate accidents or uncertainties—or even poor draughtsmanship—can be hidden by a stronger bath of acid, there is in the wood block no way out except a new start.

Wood-engraving is a dangerous craft, inasmuch as it is possible so easily to get a showy effect. The modern creative engraver has discovered that he can use the wood block as a direct means of self-expression. This is a new development, for in the last century the old professional engraver, before the invention of mechanical methods of reproduction, merely translated the artist's drawing into a wood-engraving. This has had its danger, for whereas the good artist realises that the best work is that which uses the medium to the uttermost, never abusing it, the indifferent artist is apt to excuse his careless, slovenly cutting, by saying that he is getting a " woody quality " into his work. From the one extreme of the over-grey reproductive engravings of the nineteenth century we are running into the other of the shoddy, facile, over-black prints that an ever-increasing band of young artists turn out by the hundred to-day. Only when the artist realises that he must also be a craftsman, and the craftsman aspires to be an artist, shall we preserve and develop the outstanding school of wood-engraving that is our glory to-day.